Secret SELLING TIPS

Pocket Wisdom for Sales Professionals

Bob 'Idea Man' Hooey
Author, Think Beyond the FIRST Sale

Revised and updated (2024) IngramSpark

My purpose in creating this mini-motivational book is to provide you with a positive daily dose of motivation or food for thought.

A thought which will help you focus your mind on the positive as well as on looking for new opportunities to grow, to hone your skills, gain expertise and be better equipped to serve and sell prospective customers.

A thought which will remind you to leverage your efforts in building long-term mutually beneficial relationships which generate both profitable repeat business and qualified referrals.

"At its essence, success in any selling field is a 'mental' game."
Bob 'Idea Man' Hooey

Study the top selling professionals who consistently make the most money; build the largest referral network; and generate the most repeat business; and you'll find they have conditioned their minds for success.

Selling is a series of conversations working towards gaining acceptance or generating a **'YES!"** from your prospective customer. Along the way you'll encounter a lot of **'NO's'** and a bit of negativity as well.

"The difference between the impossible and the possible lies in a person's determination." Tommy Lasorda

If you are committed to growing and succeeding in this highly competitive and changing arena, it is critical to condition yourself to remain positive and push through to win your customers commitment. You need to re-condition your mind for success.

My commitment in creating '**Secret Selling Tips – Pocket Wisdom for Sales Professionals'** is to help equip and motivate you to grow, make more money and succeed in the selling game.

Bob 'Idea Man' Hooey
Creator and guardian of The Secret Sales Tips

Reasons people buy and keep on buying

In, *"Rapid Response Advertising"* **Geoff Ayling** provides sales professionals with fifty reasons why people buy. Knowing 'why' people make purchases will allow you to position and continually re-position yourself and your company to help them do so. These tips will give you an edge to retaining them as long-term clients and repeat buyers.

See how many of Geoff's reasons already align or fit with your product and service offerings.

Discuss how you might adapt, amend, adapt, or add on to what you currently offer to make yourself a more attractive resource for meeting your client's needs over a longer period. This is one of the secrets of getting repeat business: give your client a valid reason to do so! Perhaps give them more than one!

How about 50 plus reasons! Geoff told me people make purchases for these, among other reasons:

- To make more money
- To become more comfortable
- To attract praise
- To increase enjoyment
- To possess things of beauty
- To avoid criticism
- To make their work easier
- To speed up their work
- To keep up with the Joneses
- To feel opulent
- To look younger
- To become more efficient
- To buy (some just like to shop)
- To avoid effort
- To escape or avoid pain
- To protect their possessions
- To be in style
- To avoid trouble
- To access opportunities
- To express love
- To be entertained

- To be organized
- To feel safe
- To conserve energy
- To be accepted
- To save time
- To become more fit and healthy
- To attract the opposite sex
- To protect their family
- To emulate others
- To protect their reputation
- To feel superior
- To be trendy
- To be excited
- To communicate better
- To preserve the environment
- To satisfy an impulse
- To save money
- To be cleaner
- To be popular
- To gratify curiosity
- To satisfy their appetite
- To be individual
- To escape stress
- To gain convenience
- To be informed
- To give to others
- To feel younger
- To pursue a hobby
- To leave a legacy

Sam Deep and **Lyle Sussman**, who wrote '*Close the Deal*' taught the importance of pain and the ways to learn where it resides. If you know that exactly, you've got a great starting point for your sales and creativity.

Now that you've got 50 plus ways to win the hearts and business of your prospects, you'll have an easier job of winning sales, repeat sales, and increased profits. *Excerpted from* **Think Beyond the FIRST Sale** *by Bob 'Idea Man' Hooey www.SuccessPublications.ca*

A few thoughts to succeed in business (sales)

When all is said and done, there are essentially three simple (although not necessarily easy) ways to increase your business (sales).

Work to increase the number of clients you attract to visit (in person or on-line) and retain to deal with you.

Work to increase the average size of the sale for each client.

Work to increase the frequency or number of times each client returns and buys from you again.

If you really want to **'SUCCEED in Business'**, you need a solid, easily followed process that allows you to strategically work on each of these three key areas.

Each key area will have its own challenges and opportunities for growth.

Look for innovative, virtual ways to **attract more clients** in the services and product mix you offer. Like the comparison of having a single line in the water or having multiple lines with different baits. Which one will have the best chance of catching more fish? What kinds of bait do you have? Hmmm?

How about looking for ways to add-on or cross sell? **Adding-on** helps move the client to a larger or superior product, package, or service. It is based on really understanding the intended use and realizing the basic product or service will fail to meet the real needs of your client. Help them chose wisely!

Cross selling introduces your client to additional products or service. Offer them alternatives that perform better and are in 'their' best interest. For example, phone providers do this well with bundling: Voice mail, call waiting, auto call back, 2nd line, autodial, calling cards, caller ID, 3rd line for security, internet, cable, and computer information delivery systems. Expand!

Test your offerings, product mix, and services offered. Experiment with your website, advertising, promotional materials, sales, and direct mail letters, live and **virtual** sales presentations, and in store/**virtual** demos, guarantees, USP's,

5

pricing points, volume purchase and discounts, or accessible financing. Keep refining until you find something that is more effective and then update it as needed to keep it fresh and relevant to the changing marketplace and client needs.

Look for opportunities to form **strategic alliances** with those companies who are already dealing with the people you would like to attract; those companies who have already earned their trust and respect. If you offer *complimentary*, non-competitive services or products that assist them in serving 'their clients', you will find a more favorable response. Look for opportunities to offer this kind of connection to people who want to deal with your clients and who offer something you don't offer or are unable to do so profitably at this moment.

Together we are better!

Condition your mind to look for break-through ideas and creative solutions. Investigate other industries, look at their success stories and best practices and see if they hold a secret that you can transfer to yours. For example: Fed-Ex simply copied the central distribution system used by the banking system for courier delivery. Fred did ok with this transplanted break-through idea!

As fellow author **Jay Abraham** says*, "Break throughs let you out-think, out-leverage, out-market, out-sell, out- impact, out-defend, out-maneuver, and continuously outwit your competition at every level."*

Look for **breakthrough/transferable ideas** in marketing, innovation, creativity, operations, sourcing, technology, virtual services, systems, process, selling, financing, product mix, service list, and distribution. Now is the time to grow!

In the pages that follow, you will find food for thought and perhaps a small dose of motivation to help in keeping positive and focused and profitable.

Read and think about one each day and use it to focus your attention on expanding your client base and getting new and repeat sales.

"You don't get paid by the hour. You get paid for the value you bring to the hour." Jim Rohn

A wise sales professional once told me *"I would get paid in direct proportion to the value or solutions I provided my customers."* That is even more critical for you today during global competition for business.

Customers perceive value as a reason to purchase for you. If the value is higher than the price, you gain the sale. If not, go for a walk.

As a professional salesperson the value you bring to both your prospective customers and your company is in direct proportion to what you are able to provide. Provide both with value you will become a selling superstar.

Provide mediocre value and you will create an opportunity to try another profession. Bring value and commitment to every day.

"Life isn't about what you can have: It is about what you have to give." Oprah Winfrey

How do you define or measure success? Is it simply what you have, earn, or possess? Or is it what you share, what you learn, or what you bring to the table each day that creates lasting value and substantial success?

Look at each day as an opportunity to grow and hone your skills in better serving your prospective customers. Look at each encounter as the opportunity to give your customer your absolute best in service, expertise, and advice in solving their challenges.

Did you give them your undivided attention? Did you give them the best advice and direct their search to the best product or service for them? Did you give them the opportunity to say 'YES'?

Then, you can count this day a success!

"Success seems to be connected with action. Successful people keep moving. They make mistakes, but they don't quit." Conrad Hilton

Study top performing selling professionals throughout the generations, and you will find this to be true. They are constantly moving ahead, learning, and applying those lessons to garner additional success.

Taking time to think is important. Moving ahead on those thoughts in creating Ideas At Work is where success occurs. Acting on your commitment to being professional to qualify more carefully, to asking for the order, is where you make major strides in your success.

Today you will have the opportunity to gain expertise and experience. Take it! Today you will gain the opportunity to help people buy from you. Take it! Take action and create success in your selling efforts.

"The difference between a successful person and others is not a lack of strength, not a lack of knowledge; but rather a lack of will." Vince Lombardi

Are you serious about becoming or remaining a million-dollar sales professional? Are you serious about becoming a top performer in your company or field?

Really? What have you done today to move that successfully prove that commitment to your success?

When you encounter challenges, rejection, frustration, and other *'normal'* obstacles, it will be your will to preserve, to follow through that will help keep you focused and on track for success. This is where you prove, for yourself, just how committed you are to succeeding. This is where you prove how professional you really are in this highly competitive field.

"You see things; and you say "Why?" But I dream things that never were and I say, "Why not?" George Bernard Shaw

Dream big dreams and don't concern yourself about those who don't share them. Being a visionary in the selling game is your key to long term growth and success.

Challenge yourself to stretch, to move past your comfort zone into the winner's zone. Ask yourself **'Why not?'** when it comes to seeing, setting, and achieving big goals.

Why not become that million-dollar selling professional or your company's top performer? Why not become a leader in the selling field and be the one that others look to for guidance and advice?

The only thing stopping you from answering these questions is 'you'. So, 'Why not' be the best-selling professional you can?

"You will make more friends in a week by getting yourself interested in other people than you can in a year by trying to get other people interested in you." Arnold Bennett

One of the secrets in life, business, and especially in sales is this: "All things being equal, people prefer to deal with people the like and trust."

If you want to bring your sales and selling expertise to the next level start making sure that you are *genuinely* interested in the people you would hope to serve. People know instinctively if you are really interested in them and their concerns. They can also tell when you are primarily interested in just the sale.

Long-term success and growth in the selling game is based on referrals and repeat business. They are directly influenced by how people relate to you. Enough said!

"The difference between the impossible and the possible lies in a person's determination." Tommy Lasorda

At its essence, success in any selling field is a mental game. Study the selling professionals who consistently make the most money, build the biggest referral network and generate the most repeat business and you'll find they have conditioned their minds for success.

Selling is a series of conversations working towards gaining acceptance or generating a 'YES' from your prospective customer. Along the way you encounter a lot of 'NO's' and perhaps a bit of *unpleasant* negativity too.

If you are committed to growing and succeeding in this competitive and changing arena, it is important to condition your mind for success. It is also important to condition it to remain positive while encountering the 'NO's.

"You will miss 100 percent of the shots you never take." Wayne Gretsky

How often will you suggest moving to the next step, to completing the order or the sale? How often will you take the risk and *ask* for the sale?

As many times as it takes would be the answer from generations of selling professionals. Too many salespeople starve or at best earn a mediocre income because they are **'ask resistant'**.

Would you desire to double your sales and commissions? Simply look for opportunities to ask for the order on a repeated basis. If you believe in your product or service, you do your prospective customer a disservice when you fail to give them the opportunity to do business with you and to purchase or invest in what you have to offer.

Ask them often!

"Be of good cheer. Do not think of today's failures, but of the success that may come tomorrow. You have set yourselves a difficult task, but you will succeed if you preserve; and you will find a joy in overcoming obstacles. Remember, no effort that we make to attain something beautiful is ever lost." Helen Keller

Each day, as selling professionals, we have the choice to focus on what worked instead of what did not. Those who would be the best look for lessons and move ahead to create additional opportunities for success. If a customer does not purchase today, who says, if properly treated, they will not return to buy another day.

Never let a day go without learning. However, never start a day dwelling on the failures of the days long past. Start each day with a positive sense of expectation, of success in the making. You'll win in the end and today is that day!

"Nothing is so often irretrievably missed as dialing opportunity." Marie von Ebner-Esdhenbach

Today, many opportunities for success will pass your way. Will you be ready to capture them as they come along? Will you recognize them as they do?

Each phone call, each prospective customer that you encounter is an opportunity to serve and to demonstrate your commitment to being a selling professional. Each encounter is an opportunity to help a customer define, find, and apply a solution which makes their life or business better. Each encounter is an opportunity for you, as a selling professional, to grow and to hone your skills and expertise.

Will you be ready? Are you committed to success? Are you committed to serving your customers to the best of your abilities?

"If you work just for the money, you'll never make it. But if you love what you are doing, and always put the customer first, success will be yours." Ray Kroc

Selling can be an extremely rewarding game financially, more so than many careers. Interestingly enough, the top performers don't focus on the money as a major part of their concerns.

Top performers focus on one thing in particular: *"What can I do to help this customer select the best product or service that best meets their needs and reflects their budget?"*

They've learned that ensuring they take care of the customer helps take care of the money too. Perhaps you've forgotten this on occasion and found yourself with reduced sales. Refocus your energies on profitably serving your customers and the commissions will flow.

"What you get by achieving your goals is not as important as what you become by achieving your goals." Zig Ziglar

One of the reasons we challenge you to set big goals that, if attained, would blow your mind is based on this simple truth. What you get is less important than what you become and/or what you learn in the process.

From experience, we know that you will become more professional, more focused, more disciplined, and perform at a higher level if you set personal goals that stretch you.

We also know, from experience, that in doing so you will make more money, build better long-term customer relations, gain more repeat business, and generate more referrals. Which is more important, the goal or the pursuit of the goal?

The answer is yours to discover.

"We are not in a position in which we have nothing to work with. We already have capacities, talents, direction, missions, and callings." Abraham H. Maslow

Are you just starting in the selling profession, or struggling to make it pay? That is ok.

One of the easiest things new or inexperienced salespeople do is underestimate their own skills, talents, and passions. Perhaps you've just started in your learning curve as a selling professional. Bring your experiences as a customer to your desire to learn and become more expert in serving your customers. They are just like you, and you can build on that bridge.

Many of the top performers over the generations started with no sales or product experience. They were driven to learn and found that learning directly impacted their abilities to earn. Bring your passion to perform to work with you every day.

"The three great essentials to achieving anything worthwhile are: first, hard work, second, stick-to-it-iveness, and third, common sense." Thomas Edison

Does that make sense to you? Are you applying those essentials in your growth as a selling professional?

Selling can be a very rewarding career. It is one that requires you to do your homework in preparation to serve customers. It is also one that requires your ability to stick in there in the face of rejection or lack of sales.

More importantly, it requires common sense applied to both your role as a profitable selling professional and more so in effectively serving your customers. Remind yourself that today you will do what is required, to stick in there and provide solid, trusted service and advice to your prospective customers.

"The way to get started is to quit talking and begin doing."
Walt Disney

Do you really want to be a success in the field of selling? Do you really want to become a top performer in your company?

Then stop dreaming about it. Stop talking about it or complaining about the things outside your control. Stop talking and begin doing something about it today!

Like what? **Here's an idea**: Why not make the *extra* effort to ask more qualifying questions before you lead your customer to a specific item you hope they'll purchase. Perhaps you can move past your normal fears and boldly ask for the order a minimum of three times as the opportunities present themselves.

Perhaps you can approach your company's top performers and offer to buy them lunch in an effort to learn how they succeed?

"The will to win, the desire to succeed, the urge to reach your full potential… these are the keys that will unlock the door to personal excellence." Eddie Robinson

What will you do today to further your growth and success in this competitive business? What will you do to accelerate your learning curve to ensure you are on the top of your game?

Only what you decide to do and then actually get off your chair and do! Many salespeople think about what they need to do to succeed. Most of us know the secrets. Those who become the top performers have the will to succeed and have used that will to push themselves further along the path to success.

Wanting to do something is a good start, but it is only when you commit your willpower to making it happen that you will succeed.

"Only those who will risk going too far can possibly find out how far one can go." T.S. Elliot

How far can you go in your selling career? How much money can you make each year? Are there limits to your abilities and potential?

In truth, you will never know the answers to any of these questions until you have moved past your comfort zone and pushed past where you are at the present.

Until Roger Bannister broke the 4-minute mile the world's 'experts' said it couldn't be done. The same was said about putting a man on the moon.

Your success, your career, and your long-term profitability have limits often set by you. Give it a try, see if you can push your   limits substantially. You'll surprise yourself at how far you can go once you start moving.

"Pearls lie not on the seashore. If thou desirest one thou must dive for it." **Chinese Proverb**

What is the difference between a vending machine and a selling professional? The selling profession realizes that they have a definite part to play in the sales process and impact their success by how well they play that part.

Selling professionals know that, at times, sales will take time and that they will have to work to earn the trust and business of their customers. Sure, sometimes people just come in and buy – but any vending machine minded person can take an order.

The true selling professional is not afraid to dig to find out the real motivations and needs of their customers. They are not afraid to offer additional items or up-sell something that better serves their customers.

"You were born to win; but to be a winner, you must plan to win, prepare to win, and expect to win." **Zig Ziglar**

How do you respond to Zig's statement? Do you believe it, or at least hope it is true in your case?

Selling is a *mental* game and in as much it requires you to maintain a positive focus in the outcome of your efforts. If you remain positive, you will preserve and find success where your counterparts quit and spend their time complaining and blaming.

I believe you can be as successful as you make up your mind to be. The corollary to that, is once your mind is made up, you must get up and start creating the vision in your mind. That is what the pros do!

"The man (or woman) who can drive themselves further once the effort gets painful is the one who will win." **Roger Bannister**

Sales is, as previously said, a mental game. At times, you will become tired or fatigued and need a break. At times, you will need to drive through that fatigue to fulfill your commitment to be a selling professional.

This is where you prove your commitment to yourself as well as your customer and your company. This is where you separate yourself from those who only want to succeed in this selling business. This is where you amaze yourself when the reserves are used up and you preserve to win.

Study the top performers in any industry and you'll find they have disciplined themselves to persevere in spite of pain or detours along their path. They persevere and they win.

"The most splendid achievement of all is the constant striving to surpass yourself and to be worthy of your own approval."
Denis Waitley

Have you ever amazed yourself? Have you ever stepped back and said, *"Where did I learn to do that?"*

In truth, the only person you must surpass is yourself. The only person you must really impress is yourself.

What have you done lately that surprised you or amazed you? What have you done that is so past your comfort zone that you were absolutely overwhelmed at your success in achieving it?

If you have no answers to these questions, perhaps you have been playing it safe and not pushing yourself to take risks and to grow in your career as a selling professional.

If you want to win, surpass yourself today.

"Keep away from people who try to belittle your ambitions. Small people always do that, but the really great ones make you feel that you too, can become great." **Mark Twain**

This is a touchy subject for many in sales. Very few people understand what we do and how challenging it can be to succeed. Our families often undervalue the work we do, and our colleagues are not always supportive.

Do you have people like this in your life? Avoid them when you can and remind yourself that they are entitled to their opinion, just as you are entitled to your dreams and ambitions.

Find supportive people who will encourage you in your pursuit to succeed. They exist, and they might be in the same profession (sales) with another company. Seek them out and ask for their support. Offer yours to encourage them in return. Create a success team!

"I am here for a purpose and that purpose is to grow into a mountain, not shrink to a grain of sand. Henceforth will apply all my efforts to become the highest mountain of all and I will strain my potential until it screams for mercy." **Og Mandino**

Why are you in sales? What is your purpose? Are you there to be a mediocre performer, barely surviving or making quota each month? Are you there to earn enough to pay your bills?

Or are you there because you believe you have skills, talents, and a passion to help people enrich their lives, businesses, and homes? Are you committed to success in serving your customers and in helping them make intelligent decisions, with your help?

Knowing your purpose and being committed to seeing it fulfilled works wonders in keeping you motivated and focused on success.

"I will! I am! I can! I will actualize my dream. I will press ahead. I will settle down and see it through. I will solve the problems. I will pay the price. I will never walk away from my dream until I see my dream walk away: Alert! Alive! Achieved!"
Robert Schuller

Wow! Say this to yourself every day before you walk on the sales floor or make that first call. Bet something magically happens!

Reinforcing your goals, your commitments and your positive energy with positive self-talk is a technique used very successfully by top performing sales-people as well as athletes. Being open to talk to yourself in a positive, firm, and focused manner will work miracles.

Promise yourself that, for today, you will stretch and grow and be the best-selling professional you know how. Promise yourself that you will never quit your dream to succeed.

"My advice is to go into something and stay with it until you like it. You can't like it until you obtain expertise in that work. And once you are an expert, it's a pleasure." **Milton Garland**

Look at those in your company who are the top performers. They make it look so easy, don't they? They seem to have the gift of the gab and always seem to have the right answers for the questions and objections their customers bring up, don't they?

They have invested years to learn how to do what they do. They have reflected on years of interaction with customers and applied that wisdom to serving current ones. They have invested years reading, studying, attending training programs to become better in their chosen profession.

You can too! Today is your day to choose.

"The greater danger for most of us is not that our aim was too high and we miss it, but that it is too low and we hit it." **Michelangelo**

How big is your goal this year? Is it bigger than last year? Is it bigger than the one your manager or the company helped set for you? Does it scare you or excite you?

Internally, we have a goal we can live up to or down to. You may have set something big, but unless you believe there is a chance to make it real, your subconscious mind will undermine your efforts.

Setting easily attained goals is a cheap shot at our potential. It devalues us as professionals and our abilities.

Setting a goal that makes you sweat and stretch is a good thing. Regardless of the outcome you will have grown in its pursuit and become more successful for your efforts.

"Something in human nature causes us to start slacking off at our moment of greatest accomplishment. As you become successful, you will need a great deal of self-discipline not to lose your sense of balance, humility, and commitment." **H. Ross Perot**

Don't quit, don't slow down, don't look back. Ever seen a track and field event where someone was winning and slacked off, only to see a competitor sneak by on the inside?

That happens in sales too. We are doing so well, having a good month and then we slack off. After all, we've hit our quota, haven't we?

This is a dangerous point for anyone who wants to be successful in this business. The top professionals know the best time to sell is when you are already selling and being successful.

When you slack off, you minimize your true potential and that devalues your success.

The golden opportunity you are seeking is in yourself. It is not in your environment; it is not in luck or chance, or in the help of others; it is in yourself alone." **Orison Swett Marden**

Many of us entered the selling profession because we saw it as an opportunity to do something different, to gain more control over our time and efforts and to create a better income based on our own efforts. Did you?

The opportunity for success you seek resides inside you. It is directly related to how well you succeed with your customers and your company too. Too often, we look to others to create opportunities, or to open doors, or to show us the way.

All too often, the secret was hiding inside our minds and experience just waiting to be set free and to unleash our potential. Look inside first, then bring that success into reality.

"The first step is to fill your life with a positive faith that will help you through anything. The second is to begin where you are." **Norman Vincent Peale**

Selling is a mental game and as such it is important to *prime your mental pump* with thoughts and ideas that inspire and uplift you. Working in this field can be mentally challenging and having something in place which helps keep your spirits up is a survival tool.

Read positive, challenging books. Listen to recordings that encourage and equip you to succeed. Read your Secret Selling Tips on a regular basis and go back to re-read them when you have *'one of those days.'*

Find people who are positive and who are creating success in their lives and careers. Share ideas and encourage each other. Use each opportunity to start fresh.

"Let your hook be always cast; in the pool where you least expect it, there will be a fish." **Ovid**

If you are not interacting with qualified, prospective customers you will be a hungry salesperson. Just as someone who is fishing looks to keep their line in the water (where the fish are), we as professionals in the selling field need to be in front of or in contact with customers.

This can apply as we move through life and is not limited to what we do while at work. Often, we encounter potential customers in areas outside of work.

This is not to say we need to be actively 'prospecting' everyone we meet. However, it makes sense that we should remain open to share what we do and what we offer with those we meet along the path.

Success might just be in the next pond.

"Nothing in the world can take the place of persistence. Talent will not; nothing is more common than unsuccessful men with talent. Genius will not; unrewarded genius is almost a proverb. Education will not; the world is full of educated derelicts. Persistence and determination alone are omnipotent."
Calvin Coolidge

Sales success is a series of conversations leading to, we hope, a yes or an order. Persistence is one of the keys used by top performing selling professionals to open the door to success.

Did you know the average salesperson gives up after encountering a couple of rejections? Did you know the top performers preserve as often as 7 or 8 times to get the deal?

Persistence and patience are two of the critical foundations for your success in selling.

"You don't close a sale, you open a relationship if you want to build a long-term, successful enterprise." **Patricia Fripp**

Read my friend Fripp's sage words and burn them in your mind if you are serious about becoming or remaining successful in sales. Sales success is about building long-term relationships which result in referrals and repeat business.

 Too many salespeople mistake the objective as being to close the sale when that is just the beginning. Investing time getting to know your customer, building trust, and encouraging them to buy or deal with you is good. Moving past the initial sale by exploring options to move ahead in other areas or purchases is better. Gain their trust and have them become your fan or champion is the best.

Use your time wisely, leverage your investment with each customer for the long term. Buy **Think Beyond the FIRST Sale** by Bob 'Idea Man' Hooey Available from www.successpublications.ca

"I have never worked a day in my life without selling. If I believe in something, I sell it, and I sell it hard." **Estee Lauder**

Estee Lauder built a very successful company which has grown and remained viable and profitable over the years.

That company success was built on her commitment to selling what she believed in…

What do you believe in? Do you believe in the products and services you offer? If so, then leverage that belief with positive action and be open to tell the world to buy from you. If not, then quit or invest the time to ensure you are selling something you can really believe in.

Your success will be directly linked to your ability to convey confidence and competence in your customer interaction. They can tell when you don't believe what you say… They can also tell when you are sold on it!

"Most people think 'selling' is the same as 'talking'. But the most effective salespeople know that listening is the most important part of their job." Roy Bartell

Ask any of the top performers in sales and you'll be surprised to find they are not smooth talkers at all. In fact, many of them are positive but on the shy side. Surprising then, that they do so well in this competitive industry. Why?

Quite simply, they spend time asking questions and listening to what their prospective customers tell them in response to those questions. The smart selling professional uses their active listening skills to discover several things about their customers: their budget, their dreams, their desires, their wants, and their needs.

When you actively listen, you create a bond with your customers as well as determine how to best help them purchase what they need and want.

"Always be closing… That doesn't mean you're always closing the deal, but it does mean that you need to be always closing on the next step in the process." Shane Gibson

Too many 'poor' salespeople remain their because they are *'ask resistant.'* Being a top professional in this competitive field means being committed to helping the sales process through each step to a successful purchase.

At each opportunity you get to close on that step and move the process ahead. This is how you move your career into the winner's zone.

One of the biggest obstacles of salespeople is taking that risk to ask for the sale or to advance it along the path to a successful purchase.

Commit today that you will be open to closing and move the selling process ahead when the opportunity presents itself.

***"You were born to win; but to be a winner, you must plan to win, prepare to win, and expect to win."* Zig Ziglar**

How do you respond to Zig's statement? Do you believe it, or at least hope it is true in your case?

Selling is a *mental* game and in as much it requires you to maintain a positive focus in the outcome of your efforts. If you remain positive, you will preserve and find success where your counterparts quit and spend their time complaining and blaming.

I believe you can be as successful as you make up your mind to be! The corollary to that, is once your mind is made up, you must get up and start creating the vision in your mind. That is what the pros do!

***"Do the thing you fear to do and keep doing it… that is the quickest and surest way ever yet discovered to conquer fear."*
Dale Carnegie**

How are you doing in your selling? Are you doing as well as you can, or do you think you have room to grow? Is there something that is *'stopping'* you from attaining success? Is there something you find yourself shying away from doing?

Someone once told me, **'Feel the fear and do it anyway.'** This sage advice can easily apply to those of us in the selling profession who will occasionally find ourselves reluctant to ask for the appointment or the sale. Have you ever found yourself in that position?

Resolve that, for today, you will face any fears and move ahead confidently. For today, you will be braver and ask the question.

***"If you want to be successful, find someone who has achieved the results you want and copy what they do, and you'll achieve the same results."* Michael Power**

Want to learn the secrets of the sales superstars? Want to move your sales into the million-dollar levels? Want to become one of the top sales performers?

Invest time and ask them to teach you or show you what they do when they work with a client. Be open to observe and learn from someone who is demonstrating their professionalism in serving customers and whose commissions and results give testimony to their success.

"Success leaves clues," someone once said. One of the best ways to become a success is to watch, learn and apply lessons from those who are successful.

"I am not judged by the number of times I fail, but by the number of times I succeed. The number of times I succeed is in direct proportion to the number of times I can fail and keep on trying."
Tom Hopkins

In sales we hear the word 'no' repeatedly, don't we? All too often, we work to provide service and information to find a customer deciding to 'NOT' deal with us. This can be a challenge in being a selling professional.

Too many salepeople stop short of success or gaining the trust and business of a customer because they feel like they failed. They retire to the 'loser's lounge' where their fellow non-performers commiserate with them and help them feel worse.

Get up and take another shot at success. Say to yourself, *"Next time I will do it differently. Next time I will preserve until I succeed.!"*

"One reason so few of us achieve what we truly want is that we never direct our focus; we never concentrate our power. Most people dabble their way through life, never deciding to master anything." **Anthony Robins**

Do you want to be a top performing selling professional? Don't dilute your energies or focus while at work. Don't allow yourself to be distracted by lower performers who want to complain or just waste your selling time by talking about the weather, or sports, or...

You are here today ready to do your job to the best of your abilities. That means you have less time to chat and waste if you are to gain success today.

That means disciplining yourself to focus on those activities which either make you more money or make you better in your role.

"Internalize the Golden Rule of sales that says, "All things being equal, people will do business with, and refer business to, those people they know, like and trust." **Bob Burg**

Ever wonder why some of your counterparts in the sales field seem to do more business and have more referrals? *"Gee, what are they doing that I'm not?"* might be a question to ask yourself. Perhaps they are working at showing genuine concern and befriending their customers as they experience a series of conversations during the sales process.

If you don't like people, then now is the time to polish your resume.

Selling is a personal business and very much one in which you are more effective in dealing with or influencing people when you express genuine concern for their welfare.

Be a friend, be a professional, and succeed.

"Be open to learning new lessons, even if they contradict the lessons, you learned yesterday."Ellen Degneres

Generations of top selling professionals have proven the value of remaining open to new ideas, new lessons and new methods or techniques to better do their jobs. They know they still have much to learn and for the real sales leader, **'School is never out!'**

Regardless of your experience or expertise in your field it is important to remain open to learning and to grow. Only by continual growth can you move your career productively ahead.

Each day you have an opportunity to learn from your experience with your customers, your colleagues, and your managers. Each day you have a chance to revisit your **Secret Selling Tips** and reflect on the lesson shared for your success. The choice is always yours!

A final note:

We hope you have found some inspiration in the words shared for each sales day. We hope too, that you have taken time to reflect on the wisdom contained and how it might apply to your sales situation and commitment to become more productive and profitable.

Now it is time to move on to the next month... go back to the beginning and start working through this mini-motivational pocket wisdom book again, or order one of the latest ones in our on-going series.

Added a few more ideas to complete our time together. Enjoy!

Wishing you success along the path to becoming or remaining a top performing selling professional.

Bob 'Idea Man' Hooey

Little hinges swing big doors

As I travel the globe, I share a few basic ideas or messages with my audiences. I often tell them, *"Once people fully understand the 'Why?' (purpose) the 'How's?' (processes or procedures) tend to take care of themselves."* Simple little idea, isn't it? However, these little things seem to slip the grasp of many of our North American sales leaders. We tend to over-complicate things.

W. Clement Stone, who built a billion-dollar *sales* organization out of the depths of the great depression (*early 1900's*) shared a *key* quote that has been close to my own growth and success.

He worked with **Napoleon Hill**, who authored, *Think and Grow Rich*, published *Success Magazine*, and mentored **Og Mandino**, who authored motivational classic, ***The Greatest Salesman in the World.*** **(Buy this book and apply it!)**

Stone wrote: ***"Little hinges swing big doors."***

Entrepreneurial sales leaders constantly search and are open to finding the next '*slight edge*,' the next profitable idea, or '*little hinge*'. I do too!

What little hinges have you applied in your life to open big doors or opportunities? What hinges have you used to leverage your sales skills and expertise to better your career, company, or community? We trust we have provided a few leverage points for you. What is next for you?

"If you are not taking care of your customer, your competitor will." *Bob 'Idea Man' Hooey*

This quote has grown legs being quoted in business magazines and even on a training room wall in South Africa.

Mistakes made by NEW, lazy, or ineffective sales staff

- Why is it that some senior or seasoned sales staff are often more effective and productive in their sales efforts?
- Why are some sales staff better at building long-term, profitable relationships that result in repeat sales and multiple referrals?

Could it be that they've learned these simple points that help them sell better and to build more profitable client relationships?

As we have previously discussed, companies and selling professionals that take good care of their clients generally retain them for an extended period.

For ineffective sales staff or newer sales personal that lack the proper training, there are some pitfalls here as well.

Lack of preparation. Someone once said that *"Success happens when opportunity meets preparedness."* Your level of preparedness directly impacts your credibility with a client and can make or break the establishment of a trust relationship. This means knowing your product or service as well as your firm's policies and procedures. It also means having a good understanding of what your competition provides in these same areas. Prepare yourself to win and work to make sure you become a trusted advisor in your client dealings.

Why is it we feel we can simply go through our life and our careers winging it or going with the flow? Why is it so few invest the time to prepare themselves to win, to grow, and to succeed?

Not listening. 90% of salespeople never listen or listen ineffectively and are subsequently doomed to frustration and lack of success in their selling activities. Active listening is the key foundation to discovering your client's current and future needs and to determining your ability to meet them. Asking questions and listening carefully through the interview or qualification part of the conversation is where you build solid foundations for later sales success.

I remember being interviewed by a national Canadian magazine on sales and being asked many questions about closing, overcoming objections, and such. I told the interviewer that, *"...most of the situations they presented (examples mentioned by the interviewer) could be dealt with by more effective qualifying. Ask questions earlier in the sales conversation and listen to what your clients tell you. Their answers will provide the guidance you need to help them make effective buying decisions."*

Failing to ask for the order. This is the most critical part of your sales conversation. Yet, most of the studies I've read show that 70% of all salespeople never ask for the order. A larger percentage never ask for additional orders. Do you?

I remember asking a group of home furnishing salespeople in Wisconsin, *"Would you like to learn how to double or even triple your sales income in the next year?"* Hands went up across the auditorium. I paused for dramatic effect and told them the secret, *"Simply ask for the order at least twice in the sales conversation."* I went on to say, *"Most of you are not asking even once!"* They were visibly shocked. One of their leading saleswomen told me afterwards that I was right on the money.

Poor or no follow up. Follow up and follow through is where 90% of all great sales are made. Conversely, this is where most sales staff miss the opportunity to gain and maintain a client. This is where the real sale begins (post purchase) and the relationship is built for long-term profitability.

I am continually surprised at how few salespeople follow up on leads or even keep in touch with current clients. A simple act of keeping in touch could provide the leverage to a long and mutually beneficial relationship.

Small Thinking. Want bigger sales? You must think bigger. Ask these questions: *"How high is too high? What is my maximum potential? What is the life-time value of my relationship with this client? What is the potential for referrals from this client?"*

Think big and act accordingly to see your sales results soar. Dream it and then move confidently ahead to create foundations under your dreams.

Failing to establish and/or maintain rapport. This can be a killer if you have any aspirations of maintaining a mutually profitable relationship over a long period with your clients.

Investing time, at the beginning of your sales conversation, is crucial to your success. Building on that rapport by keeping in touch can separate you from the lackluster salespeople in your field. It will also help attract clients who will become active cheerleaders and champions on your behalf.

Failing to commit and establish oneself as an expert in your field. People like to deal with (and talk about) people who know what they are doing. Failing to present yourself as such negatively impacts or restricts your future earnings with clients.

Do your homework so you know your products, services, and your industry. People love to work with people who know what they are doing and who earn their trust by their demonstrated expertise and credibility. A bit of study now can make a major difference in your future earnings and success.

Ask yourself how you fare in each of these above areas:

- Would you give yourself a passing mark?
- Which areas need a little work?
- How will you change what you do to make sure you give your clients the most professional service possible?

Give your sales team a chance to win by reminding them of these success tactics. Remind them to keep focused and keep working toward their goals of helping the client make a decision that is both good for the client and profitable over the long haul for the company.

How can you change and/or help your sales team make the changes necessary to become a professional salesperson/team and provide continued value-added service?

"Our greatest weakness lies in giving up. The most certain way to succeed is always to try just one more time." **Thomas Edison**

Thanks for reading 'Secret Selling Tips'

Each time I prepare to step on the stage; each time I sit down to write or in this case to re-write, I am challenged to deliver something that will be of use-it-now value to my audience/reader.

I ask myself, *"If I was reading or listening to this, what value would I be looking for?"*

As well, *"Why is this relevant to me, today?"*

Thanks for investing in yourself and this mini communication workbook. These two questions help to keep me focused and clear on my objectives. They help to remind me to dig into my experiences, stories, examples, and research to provide solid information that will be of benefit and help our readers, when they apply it, succeed. That can be an exciting challenge!

I trust we have done that for you in this updated primer to enhance your sales skills. **'Secret Selling Tips: Pocket Wisdom for Sales Professionals"** is my attempt to capture some of the lessons learned first-hand from observing and working with some tremendously effective sales professionals, leaders, and communicators, and to share them with you. I'd love to hear from you and read your success stories. If you would be so kind, please drop me a quick email at: bhooey@mcsnet.ca

Bob 'Idea Man' Hooey
2011 Spirit of CAPS recipient
Certified Virtual Presenter
www.ideaman.net;
www.BobHooey.training
www.HaveMouthWillTravel.com

About the author

Bob 'Idea Man' Hooey is a charismatic, confident leader, corporate trainer, inspiring facilitator, Emcee, prolific author, and award-winning motivational keynote speaker on leadership, creativity, success, business innovation, and enhancing team performance. Whew!

Using personal stories drawn from rich experience, he challenges his audiences to engage his **Ideas At Work!** – To act on what they hear, with clear, innovative building-blocks and field-proven success techniques to increase their effectiveness.

Bob challenges them to hone specific 'success skills' critical to their personal and professional advancement. Bob outlines real-life, results-based, innovative ideas personally drawn from 29 plus years of rich leadership experience in retail, construction, small business, entrepreneurship, manufacturing, association, consulting, community service, and commercial management.

Bob's conversational, often humorous, professional, and sometimes-provocative style continues to inspire and challenge his audiences across the globe. Bob's motivational, innovative, challenging, and practical Ideas At Work! have been successfully applied by thousands of leaders and professionals across the globe. **He now presents virtually due to the travel restrictions of our global pandemic.**

Bob is a frequent contributor to global consumer, corporate, association, trade, and on-line publications on leadership, success, employee motivation and training; as well as creativity and innovative problem solving, priority and time management, and effective customer service. He is the inspirational author of 33 plus publications, including several best-selling, print, e-books, reader style e-pubs, and a Pocket Wisdom series.

Visit: **www.SuccessPublications.ca** for more information.

Retired, award winning kitchen designer, Bob Hooey, CKD-Emeritus was one of only 75 Canadian designers to earn this prestigious certification by the National Kitchen and Bath Association.

In December 2000, Bob was given a special CAPS National Presidential award "...for his energetic contribution to the advancement of CAPS and **his living example of the power of one**" in addition to being elected to the CAPS National Board. He has been recognized by the National Speakers Association and other professional groups for his leadership contributions.

Bob is a co-founder and a past President of the CAPS Vancouver & BC Chapter and served as 2012 President of the CAPS Edmonton Chapter.

He is a member of the NSA-Arizona Chapter and an active leader in the National Speakers Association, a charter member of the Canadian Association of Professional Speakers, as well as the Global Speakers Federation (GSF), PSA Spain and the Virtual Speakers Association International. He retired (December 2013) as a Trustee from the CAPS Foundation. In 1998, Toastmasters International recognized Bob "...for his professionalism and outstanding achievements in public speaking". That August in Palm Desert, California Bob became the 48th speaker in the world to be awarded this prestigious professional level honor as an Accredited Speaker. He has been inducted into their Hall of Fame on numerous occasions for his leadership contributions.

Bob has been honoured by the United Nations Association of BC (1993) and received the CANADA 125 award (1992) for his ongoing leadership contributions to the community. In 1998, Bob joined 3 other men to sail a 65-foot gaff rigged schooner from Honolulu, Hawaii to Kobe, Japan, barely surviving a 'baby' typhoon en-route.

In November 2011 Bob was awarded the Spirit of CAPS at their annual convention, becoming the 11th speaker to earn this prestigious CAPS National award. Visit: www.ideaman.net/SoC.htm

Bob loves to travel, and his speaking and writing have allowed him to visit 60 countries so far. Perhaps your organization would like to bring Bob in to share a few ideas with your leaders and teams around the globe.

He is now travelling the globe virtually to deliver his programs around the globe. **He can zoom in just for you.**

Contact him at: **www.ideaman.net** bhooey@mcsnet.ca
Visit: **www.HaveMouthWillTravel.com** for more information.

Copyright and license notes

Secret Selling Tips: Pocket Wisdom for Sales Professionals *(2023)*

Bob 'Idea Man' Hooey, Accredited Speaker, 2011 Spirit of CAPS recipient.
Prolific author of 30 plus business, leadership, and career success publications

Unattributed quotations are by Bob 'Idea Man' Hooey.

Photos of Bob: **Dov Friedman**, www.photographybyDov.com
Photos of Bob: **Frédéric Bélot,** www.fredericbelot.fr/fr
Editorial, layout and design: **Irene Gaudet**, Vitrak Creative Services (a division of Creativity Corner Inc.), www.vitrakcreative.com

ISBN: 9781998014057 IS

Printed in the United States 10 9 8 7 6 5 4 3 2 1
Success Publications – a division of Creativity Corner Inc.
Box 10, Egremont, AB T0A 0Z0
www.successpublications.ca
Creative office: 1-780-736-0009

Acknowledgements, credits, and disclaimers

תודה
Dankie Gracias
Спасибо شكرا Takk
Merci
Köszönjük Terima kasih
Grazie Dziękujemy Děkojame
Ďakujeme Vielen Dank Paldies
Kiitos Täname teid 謝謝

Thank You
Tak

感謝您 Obrigado Teşekkür Ederiz
Σας Ευχαριστούμ 감사합니다
ขอบคุณ
Bedankt Děkujeme vám
ありがとうございます
Tack

As with each of my books, a very special dedication of this piece of myself, to the two people who meant the most to me, my folks **Ron and Marge Hooey.** Sadly, both my parents left this earthly realm in 1999.

To my inspiring wife, professional proof-reader and publications coach, **Irene Gaudet**, who loves, encourages, and supports me in my quest to continue sharing my **Ideas At Work!** across the world. Thank you seems so inadequate for your timely work in helping make my writing and my client service better! I love the time we spend together!

My thanks to the many people who have encouraged me in my growth as a leader, speaker, salesman, and engaging trainer in each area of expertise.

To my colleagues and friends in the National Speakers Association (NSA), the Canadian Association of Professional Speakers (CAPS), and the Global Speakers Federation (GSF) who continually challenge me to strive for success and increased excellence.

To my great audiences, leaders, students, coaching clients, and readers across the globe who share their experiences and enjoyment of my work. Your positive and supportive feedback encourages me to keep working on additional programs and success publications like this updated version. My experience with you creates the foundation for additional real-life experiences I can take from the stage to the page, the classroom to the boardroom.

My thanks to a select few friends for your ongoing support and 'constructive' abuse. You know who you are. ☺

Disclaimer

We have not attempted to cite all the authorities and sources consulted in the preparation of this book. To do so would require much more space than is available. The list would include departments of various governments, libraries, industrial institutions, periodicals, and many individuals. Inspiration was drawn from many sources, including other books by the author; in this updated creation of 'Secret Selling Tips.'

This mini-book is written and designed to provide information on more effective use of your time, as a life and leadership enhancement guide. It is sold with the 'explicit' understanding

Bob's Publications

Bob is a prolific author who has been capturing and sharing his wisdom and experience in printed and electronic forms for the past twenty-five plus years.

In addition to the following publications he has written for consumer, corporate, professional associations, trade, and on-line publications.

He has also been engaged to write and assist on publications by other writers and companies.

He loves seeing his Ideas At Work!

Leadership, business, and career development series

Running TOO Fast (8th edition 2023)
Legacy of Leadership (6thd edition 2024)
Make ME Feel Special! (6th edition 2022)
Why Didn't I 'THINK' of That? (6th edition 2022)
Speaking for Success! (10th edition 2023)
THINK Beyond the First Sale (3rd edition 2022)
Prepare Yourself to Win! (3rd edition 2017)
The early years… 1998-2009 – A Tip of the Hat collection
The saga continues… 2010-2019 - A Tip of the Hat collection (2020)

Bob's Mini-book success series

The Courage to Lead! (4th edition 2024)
Creative Conflict (3rd edition 2024)
THINK Before You Ink! (3rd edition 2017)
Running to Win! (2nd edition 2017)
Generate More Sales (5th edition 2023)
Unleash your Business Potential (3rd edition 2023)
Maximize Meetings (2024)
Learn to Listen (4th edition 2020)
Creativity Counts! (2nd edition 2024)
Create Your Future! (3rd edition 2024)
Get to Yes! *Idea-rich introductions to subtle art of creative persuasion in sales and negotiation (2023)*

Bob's Pocket Wisdom series

Pocket Wisdom for Speakers (updated 2024)
Pocket Wisdom for Leaders – Power of One! (updated 2024)
Pocket Wisdom for Innovators (updated 2024)
Pocket Wisdom for Business Builders – My Next Million Dollar Idea
Pocket Wisdom for Sales Professionals – Secret Selling Tips

Quick reads (2017-2020) - more to come in 2024

LEAD! *Idea-rich leadership success strategies*
CREATE! *Idea-rich strategies for enhanced innovation*
TIME! *Idea-rich tips for enhanced performance and productivity*
SERVE! *Idea-rich strategies for enhanced customer service*
SPEAK! *Idea-rich tips and techniques for great presentations*
CREATIVE CONFLICT *Idea-rich leadership for team success*
SUCCEED! *Idea-rich strategies to succeed in business, despite global disruptions (2020)*
WRITE ON! *Idea-rich tips and techniques to bring your book into pixels or print (2020)*

Co-authored books created by Bob

Quantum Success – 3 volume series (2006)
In the Company of Leaders (95th anniversary Edition 2019)
Foundational Success (2nd Edition 2013)
PIVOT To Present: *Idea-rich strategies to deliver your virtual message with impact (2020)*

Visit: www.SuccessPublications.ca for more information

Editor's note: Pocket Wisdom for Sales Professionals was the 1st in a series. I created an online, bi-weekly sales program for a client. A couple of months after we implemented it, he called me and told me I had to come with him to Chicago. He met with 9 other executives (similar sized companies) 3 times a year to exchange best ideas. According to him, "Secret Selling Tips was his best idea to date." I booked my flight and hotel and quickly created a slide presentation and spent a week creating our 1st pocket sized book to give to each leader.

At the end of my presentation, I offered them an incentive. If they signed up their entire sales-team, I would give them a personalized copy of SST for each salesperson. I left with 5 new clients and thousands of new sales professionals to serve. And the rest is history. Sometimes selling is serving!

What they say about Bob 'Idea Man' Hooey

As I travel across North America, and more recently around the globe sharing my **Ideas At Work!,** I am fortunate to get feedback and comments from my audiences and colleagues who gave me the gift of listening.

These comments come from people who have been touched, challenged, or simply enjoyed themselves in one of my live or virtual sessions.

I'd love to come and share some ideas with your organization and teams.

Visit: www.ideaman.net or www.BobHooey.training for more information

"I've known Bob for several years and follow his activities in business with interest. I originally met Bob when he spoke for a Rotary Leadership Institute and got to know him better when he came to Vladivostok, Russia to speak to our leadership. When you spoke I thought you were one of us because you talked about our challenges just like yours. You could understand the others, which makes you a great speaker!" **Andrey Konyushok**, Rotary International District 2225 Governor 2012-2013, far eastern Russia

"I still get comments from people about your presentation. Only a few speakers have left an impression that lasts that long. You hit a spot with the tourism people." **Janet Bell**, Yukon Economic Forums

"We greatly appreciate the energy and effort you put into researching and adapting your keynote to make it more meaningful to our member councils.
Early feedback from our delegates indicates that this year's convention was one of our most successful events yet, and we thank you for your contribution to this success." **Larry Goodhope**, Executive Director Alberta Association of Municipal Districts and Counties

"Thank you Bob; it is always a pleasure to see a true professional at work. You have made the name 'Speaker' stand out as a truism - someone who encourages people to examine their lives and make adjustments. The personal stories you shared with your audience made such a great impression on everyone. The comments indicated you hit people right where it is important - in their hearts. Each of those in your audience took away a new feeling of personal success and encouragement." **Sherry Knight**, Dimension Eleven Human Resources and Communications

"Bob is one of those rare individuals who knows how to tackle obstacles in life to reach his dreams. He takes each as a learning experience and stretches for more. His compassion and genuine interest in others make him an exceptional coach."
Cindy Kindret, Training Manager, Silk FM Radio

"Without doubt, I have gained immeasurable self-assurance. Bob, your patience and your encouragement has been much appreciated. I strongly recommend your course to anyone looking for self-improvement and professional development." **Jeannie Mura**, Human Resources Chevron Canada

"I am pleased to recommend Bob 'Idea Man' Hooey to any organization looking for a charismatic, confident speaker and seminar leader. I have seen Bob in action on several occasions, and he is ALWAYS on! Bob has the ability to grab his audience's attention and keep it. Quite simply, if Bob is involved - your program or seminar is guaranteed to succeed."
Maurice Laving, Coordinator Training and Development, London Drugs

"I have found Bob's attention to detail and his ability to fine tune his seminars to match the time frame and needs of the audience to be a valuable asset to our educational Program."
Patsy Schell, Executive Director Surrey Chamber of Commerce

"What a great conference. It was a great pleasure meeting with you at the Ritz Carlton, Cancun and I shall look forward to hopefully welcoming you and your family in Dublin, Ireland someday." **A. Paul Ryan**, Petronva Corporation, Dublin, Ireland

"Congratulations on the Spirit of CAPS Award. You have worked long and hard on behalf of CAPS …helped many speakers including me and richly deserve this award. Well done my friend." **Peter Legge**, CSP, Hof, CPAE

"I had the pleasure of hearing and watching Bob Hooey deliver a keynote speech several years ago when he gave a presentation at a Toastmasters International Convention. Bob impressed me greatly with his professionalism, energy, and ability to connect with his audience while giving them value. Dr. **Dilip Abayasekara**, DTM, Accredited Speaker, Past Toastmasters International President

Asking the Million Dollar Questions

What do you need?

How can I help you?

If you aren't asking these questions, you can be sure your competition is!" Bob 'Idea Man' Hooey

Bob 'Idea Man' Hooey — Collector of Wisdom & Creativity Catalyst
Copyright 2003-2011 Bob 'Idea Man' Hooey www.ideaman.net

Foundational hint: Asking the right questions, the questions that open conversations with your prospective clients are a key to your long-term success as a top performing salesperson. They are also strategic in building and enhancing any business or organization. Know what they need and design something creative to better serve them. That is where the sales magic happens.

"You don't need a big close, as many sales reps believe. You risk losing your customer when you save all the good stuff for the end. Keep the customer actively involved throughout your presentation, and watch your results improve." Harvey Mackay

www.ingramcontent.com/pod-product-compliance
Lightning Source LLC
Chambersburg PA
CBHW071532210326
41597CB00018B/2972